THE NEGRO MOTHER

AND OTHER
DRAMATIC RECITATIONS
By LANGSTON HUGHES

AYER COMPANY, PUBLISHERS, INC.

DEMC

THE

THE NEGRO MOTHER
AND OTHER
DRAMATIC RECITATIONS
By LANGSTON HUGHES

TITLES

THE
COLORED
SOLDIER

BROKE

THE
BLACK
CLOWN

THE
BIG-
TIMER

And

DARK
YOUTH

With Decorations By PRENTISS TAYLOR

AYER COMPANY, PUBLISHERS, INC.
SALEM, NEW HAMPSHIRE 03079

First Published 1931
Reprinted 1971

Reprinted from a copy in the
Fisk University Library Negro Collection

Reprint Edition 1987
AYER Company, Publishing, Inc.
382 Main Street
Salem, New Hampshire 03079

INTERNATIONAL STANDARD BOOK NUMBER:
0-8369-8925-2

LIBRARY OF CONGRESS CATALOG CARD NUMBER:
79-178476

PRINTED IN THE UNITED STATES OF AMERICA
BY
NEW WORLD BOOK MANUFACTURING CO., INC.
HALLANDALE, FLORIDA 33009

A *dramatic recitation to be done in the half-dark by a young brown fellow who has a vision of his brother killed in France while fighting for the United States of America. Martial music on a piano, or by an orchestra, may accompany the recitation — echoing softly,* Over There, There's a Rose That Grows in No-Man's Land, Joan of Arc, *and various other war-time melodies.*

THE MOOD	THE POEM
Calmly	My brother died in France — but I came back.
telling	We were just two colored boys, brown and black,
the story.	Who joined up to fight for the U. S. A.
Proudly	When the Nation called us that mighty day.

THE MOOD	THE POEM

THE MOOD

and
expectantly
with
head up,
shoulders
back,
and eyes
shining.
Quietly
recalling
the vision.
The dead
man speaks
with his
face
full of
light
and faith,
confident
that a
new world
has been
made.
Proud
and
smiling.
But
the
living,
remembering
with a
half-sob

THE POEM

We were sent to training camp, then overseas —
And me and my brother were happy as you please
Thinking we were fighting for Democracy's true reign
And that our dark blood would wipe away the stain
Of prejudice, and hate, and the false color line —
And give us the rights that are yours and mine.
They told us America would know no black or white:
So we marched to the front, happy to fight.

Last night in a dream my brother came to me
Out of his grave from over the sea,
Back from the acres of crosses in France,
And said to me, "Brother, you've got your chance,
And I hope you're making good, and doing fine —
'Cause when I was living, I didn't have mine.
Black boys couldn't work then anywhere like they can
    today,
Could hardly find a job that offered decent pay.
The unions barred us; the factories, too,
But now I know we've got plenty to do.
We couldn't eat in restaurants; had Jim Crow cars;
Didn't have any schools; and there were all sorts of
    bars
To a colored boy's rising in wealth or station —
But now I know well that's not our situation:
The world's been made safe for Democracy
And no longer do we know the dark misery
Of being held back, of having no chance —
Since the colored soldiers came home from France.
Didn't our government tell us things would be fine
When we got through fighting, Over There, and dying?
So now I know we blacks are just like any other —
'Cause that's what I died for — isn't it, Brother?"

THE MOOD	THE POEM
and	And I saw him standing there, straight and tall,
bowing	In his soldier's uniform, and all.
his head	Then his dark face smiled at me in the night —
in shame,	But the dream was cruel — and bitter — and somehow
becomes	not right.
suddenly	It was awful — facing that boy who went out to die,
fierce	For what could I answer him, except, "It's a lie!"
and	
angry.	It's a lie! It's a lie! Every word they said.
	And it's better a thousand times you're in France dead.
	For here in the South there's no votes and no right.
	And I'm still just a "nigger" in America tonight.
Then	
he sadly	Then I woke up, and the dream was ended —
recalls	But broken was the soldier's dream, too bad to be
the rows	mended.
of white	And it's a good thing all the black boys lying dead
crosses	Over There
in France.	Can't see! And don't know! And won't ever care!

A complaint to be given by a dejected looking fellow shuffling along in an old suit and a battered hat, to the tune of a slow-drag stomp or a weary blues.

Uh! I sho am tired.
Been walkin' since five this mornin'.
Up and down, and they just *ain't* no jobs in this man's town.
Answerin' them want-ads' not nary bit o' fun,
'Cause 'fore you gets there, ten thousand and one
Done beat you to de place, standin' out side de do'
Talkin' 'bout "we'll work for 50c a day, if we can't get no mo'."
And one old funny boy said, "I'll work at any price
Just only providin' de boss man is nice!"
You all out there laughin', but that ain't no joke—
When you're broke.

Last job I had, went to work at five in de mornin', or little mo'
And de man come tellin' me I better get there at fo'.
I mean four — before daylight — s'pose to've done hit yo' first stroke—
Folks sho is gettin' hard on you — just 'cause you broke.
So I say, "Mister, I ain't no sweepin' machine."
So de man say, "I'll get somebody else, then, to clean," —
So here I is, broke.

Landlady 'lowed to me last week, "Sam, ain't you got no money?"
I say, "Now, baby, you know I ain't got none, honey."
And don't you know that old woman swelled up like a speckled toad
And told me I'd *better* pay her for my room rent and board!
After all them dollars I gived her these last two years,
And she been holdin' 'em so tight till de eagle's in tears —
I wouldn't pay her a penny now if I was to croak —
Come bawlin' me out, 'cause I'm broke.
(I don't care nothin' 'bout her myself!)

Um-mm! Sign here says they wants somebody to shovel coal.
Well, ain't never done it, but for to keep body and soul
Together, reckon I'll try . . . Sho, I wants de job! Yes, sir!
Has I did it befo'? Certainly!
What I don't know 'bout shovelin' coal, ain't no mo' to know!
Willing worker? Un-uh! Yes! What's that you say?
De time is fourteen hours a day?
Well, er — er . . . how much does you pay?
Six dollars a week? Whee-ooo! You sho pays well!
You can take that job and go to ——— I hope you choke,
Even if I is broke.

But I sho been lookin' round hard lately for ways and means
O' gettin' a new winter coat, or havin' that old one cleaned.
Tried to find one o' them little elevator and switchboard jobs they used
    to have,

But they givin' 'em to school boys now and payin' just about half.
So I went down town to a hotel where I used to work at night,
And de man come tellin' me they ain't hirin' no mo' colored—just white.
I can't even get de money for to buy myself a smoke,
I tell you it's awful, when you're broke.

And I sho had a pretty gal, too, up yonder on Sugar Hill.
She bought a new hat last week and come sendin' me the bill.
I said, "Baby, you know I loves you, and all like that
But right long through here now, I can't 'ford to buy you no hat."
So when I got ready to go, I said, "I'll be seein' you soon, Marie."
And she come tellin' me, she ain't got no mo' evenings free!
I thought love was a dream, but I sho have awoke —
Since I'm broke.

'Course, you hears plenty 'bout this-here unemployment relief —
But you don't see no presidents dyin' o' grief —
All this talkin' ain't nothin' but tinklin' symbols and soundin' brass:
Lawd, folkses, how much longer is this gonna last?
It's done got me so crazy, feel like I been takin' coke,
But I can't even buy a paper — I'm so broke.

Aw-oo! Yonder comes a woman I used to know way down South.
(Ain't seen her in six years! Used to go with her, too!)
She would be alright if she wasn't so bow-legged, and cross-eyed,
And didn't have such a big mouth.
Howdy-do, daughter! Caledonia, how are you?
Yes, indeedy, I sho have missed *you*, too!
All these years you say you been *workin'* here?
You got a good job? Yes! Well, I sho am glad to see *you*, dear!
Is I married? No, all these-here girls up North is too light.
Does I wanta? Well, can't say but what I might —
If a pretty gal like you was willin', I'd bite.
You still bakes biscuits? Fried chicken every night? Is that true?

Certainly, chile, I always was crazy 'bout you!
Let's get married right now! Yes! What do you say?
(Is you lookin' at me, baby, or some other way?)
'Cause I'm just dyin' to take on that there marriage yoke.
Yes, um-hum! You sho is sweet! Can you pay fo' de license, dear?
'Cause I'm broke.

A dramatic monologue to be spoken by a pure-blooded Negro in the white suit and hat of a clown, to the music of a piano, or an orchestra.

THE MOOD	THE POEM
A gay and low-down blues. Comic entrance like the clowns in the circus. Humorous defiance. Melancholy jazz. Then defiance again followed by loud joy.	You laugh Because I'm poor and black and funny — Not the same as you — Because my mind is dull And dice instead of books will do For me to play with When the day is through. I am the fool of the whole world. Laugh and push me down. Only in song and laughter I rise again — a black clown.

THE MOOD

*A burst of
music. Strutting
and dancing.
Then sudden
sadness again.
Back bent as
in the fields.
The slow step.
The bowed head.
"Nobody knows
de trouble I've
had."
Flinching
under the whip.
The spiritual
syncopated.
Determined to
laugh.
A bugle call.
Gay, martial
music. Walking
proudly, almost
prancing.
But gradually
subdued to a
slow, heavy
pace. "Some-
times I feel
like a mother-
less chile."
Turning futilely
from one side
to the other.*

THE POEM

Strike up the music.
Let it be gay.
Only in joy
Can a clown have his day.

Three hundred years
In the cotton and the cane,
Plowing and reaping
With no gain —
Empty handed as I began.

A slave — under the whip,
Beaten and sore.
God! Give me laughter
That I can stand more.

God! Give me the spotted
Garments of a clown
So that the pain and the shame
Will not pull me down.

Freedom!
Abe Lincoln done set me free —
One little moment
To dance with glee.

Then sadness again —
No land, no house, no job,
No place to go.
Black — in a white world
Where cold winds blow.

THE MOOD

But now a harsh
and bitter note
creeps into
the music.
Over-burdened.
Backing away
angrily.
Frantic
with
humiliation
and helpless-
ness.
The music
is like
a mourn-
ful tom-tom
in the dark!
But out of
sadness
it rises to
defiance
and determina-
tion. A hymn
of faith
echoes the
fighting
"Marseillaise."

THE POEM

The long struggle for life:
No schools, no work —
Not wanted here; not needed there —
Black — you can die.
Nobody will care —

Yet clinging to the ladder,
Round by round,
Trying to climb up,
Forever pushed down.

Day after day
White spit in my face —
Worker and clown am I
For the "civilized" race.

Nigger! Nigger! Nigger!
Scorn crushing me down.
Laugh at me! Laugh at me!
Just a black clown!

Laugh at me then,
All the world round —
From Africa to Georgia
I'm only a clown!

But no! Not forever
Like this will I be:
Here are my hands
That can really make me free!

Suffer and struggle.
Work, pray, and fight.
Smash my way through
To Manhood's true right.

THE MOOD

*Tearing off
his clown's
suit, throwing
down the hat
of a fool,
and standing
forth,
straight
and strong,
in the clothes
of a modern
man, he proclaims
himself.*

THE POEM

Say to all foemen:
You can't keep me down!
Tear off the garments
That make me a clown!

Rise from the bottom,
Out of the slime!
Look at the stars yonder
Calling through time!

Cry to the world
That all might understand:
I was once a black clown
But now —
I'm a man!

*A moral poem to be rendered by a man in a straw hat with a bright band,
a diamond ring, cigarette holder, and a cane, to the music of piano or orchestra.*

THE MOOD	THE POEM
Syncopated	Who am I?
music.	It ain't so deep:
Telling his	I'm the guy the home folks call —
story	The Black Sheep.
in a hard,	
brazen,	I ran away.
cynical	Went to the city.
fashion.	Look at me now and
Careless,	Laugh — or take pity.
and half-	
defiant	I'm the bad egg, see!
echoes	Didn't turn out right.
of the	My people disowned me —
"St. James	So I'm hustlin' in the night.

THE MOOD

Infirmary"
as the music
takes
on a
blues
strain,
gradually
returning to
a sort of
barrel-house
jazz.
Showing-off.
Strutting
about
proudly,
bragging
and
boasting,
like a
cheap
bully. But
suddenly
looking ahead:
shrugging his
shoulders
at fate.
Accepting
his position —
but inside
himself un-
happy and blue.

THE POEM

Drinkin' and gamblin' now,
And livin' on gals.
Red-hot — that's me,
With a lot o' sporty pals.

Spendin' money like water.
Drinkin' life like wine.
Not livin' like I oughter,
But — ain't my life mine?

I got a high-yaller.
Got a diamond ring.
I got a furnished-up flat,
And all that kind o' thing.

I got a big car
And I steps on the gas,
And whoever don't like it
Just gimme some sass,

'Cause I carries a switch-blade
And I swing it a-hummin',
And if I don't get you goin',
I'll cut you down comin'.

You say I'll meet a bad endin', heh?
Well, maybe I will.
But while I'm livin' — I'm livin'!
And when I'm dead — I'll keep still.

I'm a first class hustler,
Rounder and sport.
Sometimes I'm settin' pretty,
And again money's short.

THE MOOD

Hiding his

discontent

as thoughts

of a

better life

overcome him.

Assuming

a false

and bragging

self-assurance,

and a

pretended

strength he

doesn't

really feel.

Gay,

loud,

unhappy

jazz.

Baring

his inner

heartaches

and loneliness

to the

ironic

gaiety of

the music.

THE POEM

But if I wanted to go straight
I'd starve and — oh, well —
I'm just a good-timer
On my road to hell.

Lots of old schoolmates are married now;
Home, kids, and everything fine.
But I aint got nothin' real
That I can call mine.

But don't let it matter to you,
 Cause I'm all right.
I'm eatin' and lovin',
And holdin' things tight.

So don't worry 'bout me,
Folks, down yonder at home.
I guess I can stand the racket
And fight it out alone.

I guess I know what I'm up against.
I don't cry over troubles.
Look 'em in the face and
Bust 'em like bubbles.

I turn on the radio,
Mix up a drink,
Make lots o' noise,
Then I don't have to think.

Call in a gang o' women
And let 'em have my money,
And forget that they lyin'
When they callin' me honey.

THE MOOD

Then
pulling
himself together,
boasting
loudly again,
but realizing
within
the tragic
emptiness
of his
life.

THE POEM

So what's the use o' worryin'
Or thinkin' at all?
We only got one life
And I guess that one's all —

So I'm takin' it easy
And I don't give a damn —
I'm just a big-timer,
That's all I am!

That's . . . all . . . I . . . am.

PT

A poem to be done by a woman in the bandana and apron of the Old South — but with great dignity and strength and beauty in her face as she speaks. The music of the spirituals may be played by a piano or an orchestra as the aged mother talks to her modern sons and daughters.

Children, I come back today
To tell you a story of the long dark way
That I had to climb, that I had to know
In order that the race might live and grow.
Look at my face — dark as the night —
Yet shining like the sun with love's true light.
I am the child they stole from the sand
Three hundreds years ago in Africa's land.

I am the black girl who crossed the dark sea
Carrying in my body the seed of the Free.
I am the woman who worked in the field
Bringing the cotton and the corn to yield.
I am the one who labored as a slave,
Beaten and mistreated for the work that I gave —
Children sold away from me, husband sold, too.
No safety, no love, no respect was I due.
A prey to white passion, a slave to white lust,
Nothing was too low for me then, in the dust.
Three hundred years in the deepest South:
But God put a song and a prayer in my mouth.
God put a dream like steel in my soul.
Now, through my children, I'm reaching the goal.
Now, through my children, young and free,
I realize the blessings denied to me.
I couldn't read then. I couldn't write.
I had nothing, back there in the night.
Sometimes, the valley was filled with tears,
But I kept trudging on through the lonely years.
Sometimes, the road was hot with sun,
But I had to keep on till my work was done:
I *had* to keep on! No stopping for me —
I was the seed of the coming Free.
I nourished the dream that nothing could smother
Deep in my breast — The Negro Mother.
I had only hope then, but now through you,
Dark ones of today, my dreams must come true:
All you dark children in the world out there,
Remember my sweat, my pain, my despair.
Remember my years, heavy with sorrow —
And make of those years a torch for tomorrow.
Make of my past a road to the light
Out of the darkness, the ignorance, the night.

Lift high my banner out of the dust.
—Stand like free men supporting my trust.
Believe in the right, let none push you back.
Remember the whip and the slaver's track.
Remember how the strong in struggle and strife
Still bar you the way, and deny you life —
But march ever forward, breaking down bars.
Look ever upward at the sun and the stars.
Oh, my dark children, may my dreams and my prayers
Impel you forever up the great stairs —
For I will be with you till no white brother
Dares keep down the children of the NEGRO MOTHER.

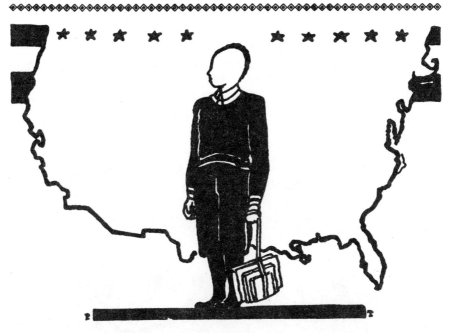

A recitation to be delivered by a Negro boy, bright, clean, and neatly dressed, carrying his books to school.

Sturdy I stand, books in my hand —
Today's dark child, tomorrow's strong man:
> The hope of my race
> To mould a place
In America's magic land.

American am I, none can deny:
He who oppresses me, him I defy!
> I am Dark Youth
> Seeking the truth
Of a free life beneath our great sky.

Long a part of the Union's heart —
Years ago at the nation's start
> Attucks died
> That right might abide
And strength to our land impart.

To be wise and strong, then, studying long,
Seeking the knowledge that rights all wrong —
    That is my mission.
Lifting my race to its rightful place
Till beauty and pride fills each dark face
    Is my ambition.

So I climb toward tomorrow, out of past sorrow,
    Treading the modern way
With the White and the Black whom nothing holds back—
    The American Youth of today.